Invite your students to join SonForce Kids—God's courageous team of disciples standing side-by-side to serve Him. As SonForce special agents, they will follow in the words of Joshua 1:9: *Be strong and courageous. Do not be terrified; do not be discouraged, for the Lord your God will be with you wherever you go.*

The SonForce Kids headquarters is located on a satellite orbiting high above the earth. In this hi-tech command center, SonForce agents gather to prepare for their five Daily Missions: Trust! Unite! Train! Follow! Lead! Throughout VBS, your students will have the opportunity to grow in their understanding of what it means to serve God with courage as they advance from Level 1 to Level 5 agents.

From the courage shown by baby Moses' family, Level 1 agents will learn to **TRUST in God's Plans.** Following Esther's example, Level 2 agents will be encouraged to **UNITE with God's People.** To help them make wise choices like Daniel did, Level 3 agents will learn to **TRAIN for God's Service.** Just as Jeremiah obeyed God even when it was difficult, Level 4 agents will learn to **FOLLOW in God's Path.** Finally, like Joshua and Caleb, Level 5 agents will get ready to **LEAD Others to God's Promises.**

So get ready for an out-of-this-world adventure. SonForce Kids—courageous kids on a mission for God!

SonForce Kids

SESSION	FOCUS	BIBLE STORY
**1** TRUST In God's Plans	**PreK/Kindergarten** We can trust in God's love for us. **Elementary** We can have courage in all situations by trusting in God's love and plans for us.	**Moses:** **Boy in a Basket** Exodus 1—2:10
2 UNITE With God's People	**PreK/Kindergarten** We can help others. **Elementary** We can have courage to stand up for others by uniting with God's people.	**Esther:** **Queen at Risk** Esther 2—8
3 TRAIN For God's Service	**PreK/Kindergarten** We can do what is right. **Elementary** We can have courage to make wise choices by training to serve God.	**Daniel:** **Servant of God** Daniel 1
4 FOLLOW In God's Path	**PreK/Kindergarten** We can obey God, even when it is hard. **Elementary** We can have courage to follow in God's path, even when it is difficult.	**Jeremiah:** **Prophet in Trouble** Jeremiah 36—39
5 LEAD Others to God's Promises	**PreK/Kindergarten** We can have courage because God promises to always be with us. **Elementary** We can have courage to lead others to God's promises.	**Joshua:** **Spy in a Strange Land** Numbers 13—14:9

BIBLE MEMORY VERSE

ASSEMBLY SKIT

PreK/Kindergarten
"Trust in the Lord." (See Jeremiah 17:7.)

Elementary
"Blessed is the man who trusts in the Lord, whose confidence is in him." Jeremiah 17:7

Mission Malfunction
Inez Halley and Jack Oort want to become Level 5 SonForce agents. They hope to impress Miss Newton with Robot's demonstration. But what is Edward Clark Felton doing with that remote control?

PreK/Kindergarten
"With love, help each other." Galatians 5:13

Elementary
"Devoted to one another in brotherly love. Honor one another above yourselves."
Romans 12:10

Asteroid Angst
An asteroid is on a collision course with Earth! But first, it threatens to smash into the SonForce Agency satellite station. Can special agent partners Inez and Jack stop it? Or will they be stuck cleaning the bathrooms?

PreK/Kindergarten
"Listen to advice and you will be wise."
(See Proverbs 19:20.)

Elementary
"Listen to advice and accept instruction, and in the end you will be wise." Proverbs 19:20

Hero Worship
Miss Newton doesn't believe Inez and Jack when they reveal that Felton is behind the asteroid threat! But now Felton realizes they're a threat to his plan to make himself a hero. What will Felton do to Inez and Jack?

PreK/Kindergarten
"Obey me, and I will be your God." Jeremiah 7:23

Elementary
"Obey me, and I will be your God and you will be my people. Walk in all the ways I command you, that it may go well with you." Jeremiah 7:23

Backdoor Breakthrough
The asteroid is minutes away from crashing into SonForce Agency! Inez and Jack know it's important to expose Felton as a fraud before anyone gets hurt. But what can they do tied up in a bathroom?

PreK/Kindergarten
"Be strong and courageous . . . for the Lord your God will be with you wherever you go." Joshua 1:9

Elementary
"Be strong and courageous. Do not be terrified; do not be discouraged, for the Lord your God will be with you wherever you go." Joshua 1:9

Remote Trouble
Oh, no! Felton thought he had everything under control, but now he can't stop the asteroid! Will Inez and Jack be able to stop it? Will Robot help? Will Felton realize what it really means to be a hero?

Helpful Hints

>> Pray for each child in your group, asking for God's help in guiding them.

>> Ahead of time, walk the route your group will take. Check entrances and exits as well as locations of restrooms and drinking fountains.

>> Check with leaders about a signal that indicates when it's time for your group to move to the next center.

>> When you arrive at a center, be prepared with a quick game in case the leader at that center is not quite ready.

>> Learn each child's name and use it often. To get a child's attention, say the child's name first. ("Tyler, it's time to sit together on the floor.")

>> Sit with your group (on the floor, at a table, etc.) and participate with children in each activity.

>> Give your attention to the children, not another guide. Treat each child as a favorite. Children who are new to the church and children who feel left out will need your special attention.

>> Focus your attention on what children are doing right. ("I like the way Corinne asked Ryan for the glue. Good work, Corinne!") Avoid mostly noticing problems.

>> When a child causes a problem, tell the child what to do, rather than what to stop doing. ("Annie, work only on your paper. Let Daniel finish his own work.") Positive guidance is better than a negative comment.

>> Help a child who is having problems getting along or following directions: Sit by the child. Separate children who don't work well together.

>> If a problem behavior continues, talk with the activity leader about how to deal with that child.

Use these ideas when you have extra time between activities or while moving from one activity to another. They are designed to be played quickly, using minimal equipment.

>> Students line up in a shape other than a straight line. Students work together to form their line into an S shape, a square, rectangle, triangle, etc. (Optional: Invite a student volunteer to choose the line shape. He or she then leads others in forming the shape.)

>> Play a game like Hot and Cold. Students sit in a circle or stand in a line. Ask a volunteer to cover his or her eyes while you hide an object somewhere in the room. Students help volunteer locate item by saying the phrase "Radar On" when the volunteer is near the item and saying the phrase "Radar Off" when he or she is farther away. Students continue until volunteer locates the item.

>> Students form a circle and number off. Student with the highest number stands in the center to act as "It." "It" taps a balloon up in the air and calls out a number. The person whose number is called tries to catch the balloon before it touches the floor. If he or she succeeds, "It" takes another turn. If he or she fails, he or she becomes the next "It."

>> To challenge students during cleanup time, play a short song from a CD. Encourage students to finish cleaning up before the song finishes.

>> Write a word on a sheet of paper. Choose a volunteer to cover his or her eyes. Show the word to the other students. Volunteer opens eyes and calls on individual students to give one-word clues to help him or her guess the word. For example, if the word is "dog," the clues might be "furry," "bark," "bone," etc. Student who gives the last clue before the word is guessed becomes "It" for the next round.

>> Pick a word whose letters can be used to form many smaller words (for example, "satellite"). Write each letter of the word on a separate index card. Give one card to each student. Students start by standing together, holding up their cards to spell the word. Students without cards then call out words that can be formed from the word (for example, "late," "sell," "eat," etc.). Students with cards then reorder themselves to spell the new word. Students repeat this process, spelling as many words as possible. Frequently switch which students hold cards.

Moses:
Boy in a Basket

Scripture
Bible Story: Exodus 1—2:10

New Testament Connection: Matthew 2:13-14

Lesson Focus
PreK/Kindergarten: We can trust in God's love for us.

Elementary: We can have courage in all situations by trusting in God's love and plans for us.

Bible Memory Verses
PreK/Kindergarten: "Trust in the Lord."
(See Jeremiah 17:7.)

Elementary: "Blessed is the man who trusts in the Lord, whose confidence is in him." Jeremiah 17:7

Enrichment Verse: "We are God's workmanship, created in Christ Jesus to do good works, which God prepared in advance for us to do." Ephesians 2:10

Teacher Devotional

Every parent knows how stressful it can be to adjust to a new baby, but the experience of Moses' family far exceeds anything most of us will ever know. The family had a beautiful new baby boy, but Pharaoh had ordered that all Hebrew baby boys be thrown into the Nile River. Imagine trying to quiet a tiny crying baby quickly enough so that soldiers wouldn't come to kill him! As Moses grew, his parents' choices were few; if he were discovered, he would die. They did have an idea, however: They put him in the Nile in a waterproof basket. They did all they could, TRUSTING God to do something miraculous.

God had big plans for Moses. He protected Moses and used him mightily. Now think about your own life. You've seen God protect you, perhaps even through some times as dangerous as those Moses faced. Pause to consider what His plans may be for you! Those plans may not look big to you—they may even be hidden from your sight right now—but rest assured, they are of eternal importance!

There are no little plans in God's eyes. What you are doing at this moment is part of the amazing tapestry He is weaving for you and through you. In His plan, your words and actions will affect many others. He has led you and protected you just as He protected Moses. Trust in God as you watch His plans unfold!

A long time ago, God's people, the Israelites, were living in the land of Egypt. Egypt was ruled by powerful kings called pharaohs. One day a new pharaoh became ruler, and he didn't like the Israelites one bit! "There are too many Israelites living here," Pharaoh told his leaders. "What if they join our enemies and fight against us?"

"You're right," the men agreed. "The Israelites are dangerous."

"Those Israelites will become my slaves," Pharaoh decided. "They will work hard from morning to night!"

Pharaoh's orders were immediately carried out. And the life of every Israelite was changed forever. The Egyptians used whips to make the Israelites work very hard. As slaves, the Israelites made enough bricks and built enough buildings to make two large cities. An odd thing happened, though: The harder the Israelites worked, the more of them there seemed to be. Pharaoh wanted to DECREASE the number of Israelites, but instead their numbers INCREASED.

Soon Pharaoh thought of another plan. He told the women who helped Israelite mothers when they were having babies that when a baby boy was born, they should KILL the baby! These women knew God would not want them to obey Pharaoh's order. They protected the baby boys instead of hurting them.

So Pharaoh gave a terrible new order. "Drown all the Israelite baby boys," he said. "Throw them into the Nile River!" One Israelite family determined they would NOT let Pharaoh kill their baby boy. For three months the family kept their baby a secret.

Soon the baby's mother had a new idea to keep the baby safe. She got a basket and used tar and pitch (a sticky material like tar) to make it waterproof. She carefully laid her baby in the basket and covered him with cloths.

The mother called to her older daughter. "Miriam, come with me." They walked down to the river. The mother carefully took the basket with the baby inside and gently placed it on the water. She turned to Miriam and said, "Hide in the tall plants by the water and watch to make sure the baby is safe." The mother went home sad and very concerned about her baby.

Miriam did exactly what her mother told her to do. She stepped back and hid in the tall plants beside the river and watched as the basket floated on the water. *What if soldiers see the basket? What if there is a crocodile nearby?* she might have wondered fearfully. Then she heard voices. Some women were coming to the river to bathe. Miriam peeked through the plants. Miriam could hardly believe her eyes! It was the PRINCESS—Pharaoh's own daughter—and her servants! *Would they see the basket? Would they call Pharaoh's soldiers?*

"That looks like a basket over there," the princess said. "Go and get it," the princess told her maid. When the princess opened the basket, the baby was crying. The princess felt sorry for him. "This is one of the Israelite babies," the princess said.

Meanwhile, Miriam was watching from her place along the river. Miriam summoned up all of her courage and stepped forward. Miriam's heart must have been beating wildly! "Would you like me to go get one of the Israelite women to take care of the baby for you?" she asked timidly.

"Yes," answered the princess, "go and do that." So Miriam ran to find someone who could take care of the baby. Miriam immediately went to her own mother and brought her back to the princess.

"Take care of this baby for me and I will pay you," the princess said to her. Now the baby was safe! No one would try to hurt a baby that belonged to the princess—and the baby got to live with his family for a while!

The baby grew to be a little boy. Soon it was time for the baby to go and live in the palace with the princess. The princess named him "Moses," which in Egyptian means "is born." The name "Moses" also sounds like the Hebrew word meaning "to draw out." His name would remind the princess, and anyone else who knew this story, that Moses was drawn or taken out of the river. Moses lived in Pharaoh's palace until he was a grown man.

Conclusion

Courage doesn't mean not feeling any fear. Courage means being willing to act, even when we ARE afraid or worried. Miriam and her mother showed courage by planning a way to keep Moses safe and then going through with their plan despite their fear. No matter how small or how big our worries or fears are, we know that because of His love for us, God has a plan for us. Because we can trust in God's love and plans, we can have courage in ALL situations.

New Testament Connection:

In Matthew 2:13-14 in the New Testament, the Bible tells of a time when Mary and Joseph had to have courage, too. An angel appeared to Joseph in a dream and told him that King Herod wanted to kill baby Jesus. God's plan was for Mary and Joseph to take Jesus to Egypt and live there until it was safe to return home. They followed God's plan even though Herod's threats may have frightened them. Mary and Joseph trusted in God's plan to keep Jesus safe. They knew that God's plans are always the best!

Esther: Queen at Risk

Scripture
Bible Story: Esther 2—8

New Testament Connection: Matthew 4:18-22; Mark 3:13-19

Lesson Focus
PreK/Kindergarten: We can help others.

Elementary: We can have courage to stand up for others by uniting with God's people.

Bible Memory Verses
PreK/Kindergarten: "With love, help each other." Galatians 5:13

Elementary: "Be devoted to one another in brotherly love. Honor one another above yourselves." Romans 12:10

Enrichment Verse: "Each of you should look not only to your own interests, but also to the interests of others." Philippians 2:4

During the rule of Xerxes (also known by the Hebrew name Ahasuerus) of Persia occurs the beautiful and charming story of Esther. Although God's name is not mentioned in the book of Esther, His presence can be found behind each word. God has a part in all the events of human life.

Esther stands out as God's chosen one. The beauty of Esther was that she wasn't spoiled by her great position. Though she became queen of a great king, she didn't forget the kindness of her cousin Mordecai, who had brought her up from childhood. Esther was faced with the opportunity to help rescue the lives of her oppressed people, the Jews, but only at great risk to her own life. Accepting this dangerous task, she carried it out with courage and wisdom. Even as she went forward on behalf of the Jews, she asked them to pray and fast on HER behalf. Esther knew that God was listening to the prayers of His people and that with His help they could UNITE and defeat their enemy.

It was a daring act for her to enter unsummoned into the presence of the king. Yet she knew she must choose the right course, despite the danger to herself. She knew this was a time to have courage and stand up for others. Esther was prepared and was brought to the kingdom for just such an hour.

We would all do well to pause and ask, "Why has God allowed me to live at this particular hour?" When faced with challenges that require the courage to do what is right, it is always easier when we are supported by the prayer of fellow believers.

Many years ago in Persia, there lived a girl named Esther. Her family had been taken as captives from their home in Israel many years before. When Esther's parents died, she lived with her cousin Mordecai (MOR-dih-ki). He cared for Esther as she grew into a beautiful young woman.

One day, the king of Persia announced that he was looking for a new queen. Esther was one of many young women chosen to come to the palace and prepare to meet the king. For a whole year, the women were given special beauty treatments. They put expensive oils and perfumes on their skin to make it soft and sweet-smelling. The women were given beautiful clothes to wear and their hair was brushed until it was shiny and smooth.

The day came for the king to meet each young woman. The women put on their best clothes and made themselves as beautiful as they could. They knew whoever pleased the king the most would become the new queen. One by one, the king met each of the young women. When Esther finally had her turn to meet the king, he was so pleased with her that he chose Esther to be the next queen!

Now about this time, the king put a man named Haman in charge of all the other government officials. Haman was so proud of his new job that he wanted everyone to bow down to him! Esther's cousin Mordecai also worked for the king. But Mordecai would NOT bow to Haman. Mordecai, like Esther, was Jewish and believed he should only bow to God. Haman was so angry that he planned to DESTROY not just Mordecai but ALL the Jewish people!

So Haman told the king lies about the Jewish people in the kingdom. He made the Jewish people sound VERY dangerous. "There are people in your kingdom who do not obey your laws. If it pleases the king, let an order be issued to destroy them! I will put a lot of money in the treasury to pay the men who do this." The king was convinced. He gave Haman permission to have these people KILLED! But the king didn't know it was the JEWS whom Haman planned to kill! And he didn't know that Esther was Jewish! Soon, Haman's horrible orders were sent all over the country!

Mordecai sent her a message and asked her to beg the king for help. After all, if Haman's plan succeeded, ALL the Jews would be killed—even Esther!

But Esther was afraid. Anyone who went to the king uninvited could be KILLED! And the king hadn't invited Esther to come and see him for a full month. Mordecai told Esther that she may have been made queen just so she could help to save her people. Esther asked Mordecai to gather all the Jews together and to fast for her. Fasting meant they would go without food and spend time in prayer. Esther told Mordecai that after they fasted she would go to talk to the king and if the king decided to kill her then so be it. Mordecai and all the Jews in the city united and fasted for three days. These three days helped Esther get ready to talk to the king.

Soon Esther was standing in the palace court. According to law, unless the king held out his scepter, Esther would be killed! *Will the king be angry I came to him uninvited?* she must have wondered anxiously. *Will he hold out his scepter to me?* The king saw her—and held out his scepter! He asked Esther what she wanted. Esther didn't tell the king what she wanted just yet. Instead, she invited him and Haman to a banquet. At the banquet, the king asked again what Esther wanted. Once more, Esther asked the king and Haman to another banquet the next day.

When the king and Haman came to the second banquet, the king asked again what she wanted. "Whatever you want, my queen, I will give to you," the king said. "Even if you ask for half of my kingdom, I will give it to you!"

"If it pleases you, O king, grant me my life," Queen Esther said. "And, please spare the lives of my people, too." Esther told about the orders that would get her and her people killed.

"Who dares threaten my queen?" the king thundered.

"It is THAT man!" Esther said and pointed to Haman.

The king was furious. He ordered that Haman be killed. Then Esther and Mordecai wrote a new law so that the Jews could protect themselves. Finally, Esther ruled that the Jewish people celebrate! Even now, Jewish people remember Esther's actions and God's power by celebrating the Feast of Purim.

Conclusion

Esther's courageous actions made a HUGE difference to her people. God can use our actions to make a difference in other people's lives, too. When we choose to be friends with people who are lonely and when we stand up for people that other kids tease, we make a difference to them. Uniting with others can give us courage to stand up for others who need help.

New Testament Connection:

In Matthew 4:18-22 and Mark 3:13-19, we read about Jesus calling 12 men to be His disciples—special agents for God! These men made a difference in the lives of other people by working together to serve God. They followed Jesus and helped Him throughout His ministry here on Earth, and continued helping people even after Jesus returned to heaven.

Daniel: Servant of God

Scripture

Bible Story: Daniel 1

New Testament Connection: Matthew 5—7

Lesson Focus

PreK/Kindergarten: We can do what is right.

Elementary: We can have courage to make wise choices by training to serve God.

Bible Memory Verses

PreK/Kindergarten: "Listen to advice and you will be wise." (See Proverbs 19:20.)

Elementary: "Listen to advice and accept instruction, and in the end you will be wise." Proverbs 19:20

Enrichment Verse: "The Lord gives wisdom, and from his mouth come knowledge and understanding." Proverbs 2:6

Imagine living through an enemy attack that destroys your home and makes you a prisoner of war. Daniel and his friends lived through just this horror, probably while they were still teenagers. The best and brightest of Jerusalem's royal court, they saw their promising futures and privileged circumstances evaporate as they left Jerusalem behind.

Captive in a strange land, they were without a country or a chosen future. The Babylonians were clearly working to eliminate their Israelite identities and make them ready to serve Nebuchadnezzar. The boys probably had no choice about being dressed in Babylonian fashion or given Babylonian names. But there was one way they could hold on to who they really were: They could honor the dietary laws of Israel. It may seem like a small thing to us, but it was one way to be obedient and remain true to the training they had received to serve God.

God often brings such small acts to our attention, acts we can do to continue to put into practice our love and obedience to God. These small acts may not seem any more significant than the food choices of Daniel and his friends. It's usually easier to ignore such small things and go along with "the program." But remembering the ways in which we have been trained will help us obey God with the courage of Daniel. When we're tempted to go along with the crowd, God gives us courage and strength to stand up for His ways like Daniel and his friends did.

Many years ago in Jerusalem, there lived four boys who were probably young teenagers. Their names were Daniel, Hananiah (han-uh-NI-uh), Mishael (MEE-shah-el) and Azariah (az-uh-RI-uh).

The armies of Babylon attacked Jerusalem, where the boys lived. Enemy soldiers took thousands of captives away—including these boys! As they left the city gates, probably tied together, they must have silently said good-bye to their schools, their families and everything they knew. They were on their way to live as slaves in the country of Babylon—probably for the rest of their lives. They would never be able to go home again.

After they arrived at the new city, the Babylonian king decided some of the Israelite slaves would serve him. He instructed his chief official, Ashpenaz (ASH-puh-nahz) to choose several young men to go into three years of training to serve him. Ashpenaz was to choose the most handsome, intelligent, strong and healthy young men from all the Israelites. Among those chosen were Daniel and his three friends. This meant that they would not be treated like slaves. That was a good thing; but there were problems, too!

The first thing that happened was everyone's name was changed. Daniel became Belteshazzar; Hananiah became Shadrach; Mishael became Meshach and Azariah became Abednego. These new names honored false gods that were worshiped by the people in Babylon.

Then came another problem. The king told Ashpenaz, "Everyone chosen to serve me must eat food from MY table!" The king may have thought this was an honor. But the king's order created a BIG problem for Daniel and his friends.

The four boys knew that in the Bible book Leviticus, God had commanded His people not to eat certain foods. Also, the king's food had probably been used for worshiping the false gods of the Babylonian people. Eating that food would be like worshiping the false gods—and if they did that, they would be dishonoring God!

If we obey the king and DO eat the food, we will disobey God, Daniel and his friends must have thought. *But if we DON'T eat the food, we will disobey the king; and he may have us killed!*

It might have seemed safest for Daniel and his three friends to go ahead and eat the king's food. They may have thought, *No one will ever know! Our parents are not here, and besides, that law is so old-fashioned*. But Daniel and his friends had been trained to serve God. They knew they should make wise choices that would please God. They knew what God said was right. And this gave them the courage they needed to do what they knew was right—NO MATTER WHAT!

"It's against the laws of our God to eat the king's food," Daniel explained to Ashpenaz. "Please ask the king if we can have only vegetables to eat and water to drink."

Ashpenaz said, "No, I won't do that. I'm afraid if you and your friends don't stay healthy, the king will be angry with me!"

But Daniel was determined to obey God. And God gave him an idea. Daniel went to the guard in charge of all the young men. "Let's try something: For 10 days, give my friends and me only vegetables to eat and water to drink. After that, compare us to the young men who eat the king's food. If we don't look stronger and healthier than the others, we'll also eat the king's food."

The guard agreed to Daniel's experiment. For 10 days, Daniel, Shadrach (SHAHD-rahk), Meshach (MEE-shahk) and Abednego (uh-BEHD-nee-goh) ate nothing but vegetables and drank only water. The rest of the young men ate food from the king's table.

At the end of 10 days, Daniel and his friends looked better than all of the other young men who ate the royal food. Instead of growing weak from not eating the food at the king's table, Daniel and his friends were strong and healthy! The guard continued to let the four friends eat vegetables and drink water.

At the end of the three years of training, Ashpenaz took all the young men to the king. The king looked at them and talked with each one; but his favorites were Daniel, Shadrach, Meshach and Abednego. God gave these four young men more wisdom than the king's own advisors.

Conclusion

Though Daniel and his friends had been chosen to train for service to the Babylonian king, they had been training to serve God all of their lives! Because Daniel and his friends had studied God's Word and knew God's rules, they had the courage to make wise choices. Knowing they were doing what would please God gave them the courage they needed to continue serving God.

New Testament Connection:

In the New Testament, we read about how Jesus trained His disciples to serve Him. Every day, as the disciples traveled with Jesus, they listened as He talked about God and how to please Him. Matthew 5—7 tells about Jesus' Sermon on the Mount, in which He gives His disciples training on how to serve God with their attitudes as well as their actions.

4 FOLLOW In God's Path

Jeremiah: Prophet in Trouble

Scripture
Bible Story: Jeremiah 36—39

New Testament Connection: Luke 22:39—24:53

Lesson Focus
PreK/Kindergarten: We can obey God, even when it is hard.

Elementary: We can have courage to follow in God's path, even when it is difficult.

Bible Memory Verses
PreK/Kindergarten: "Obey me, and I will be your God." Jeremiah 7:23

Elementary: "Obey me, and I will be your God and you will be my people. Walk in all the ways I command you, that it may go well with you." Jeremiah 7:23

Enrichment Verse: "This is love: that we walk in obedience to his commands. As you have heard from the beginning, his command is that you walk in love." 2 John 1:6

Jeremiah was called from the obscurity of his native town to assume, at a critical hour in the nation's life, the overwhelming responsibilities of a prophet. His father, Hilkiah, was a priest, so Jeremiah inherited the traditions of an illustrious ancestry. His early life was likely also influenced by strong religious leaders. But God had something even better for Jeremiah than to spend his life as a priest serving at the altar. God appointed this young man to be a prophet of the Lord in this trying hour in the history of the Chosen People.

Frequently, the Israelites chose to disobey God, even though God's commands had been designed for their well-being. When they stopped following God, they ended up in great trouble. So God warned them through Jeremiah's messages. Just as the people of Israel had to choose whether or not they would listen to the warning in Jeremiah's messages, people today face the choice between following God's ways or pursuing their own ways.

The God of Jeremiah is always ready to give each one of us, and the children we teach, the courage we need to follow in His path, even in difficult circumstances. God's promise of courage springs from His love. He is ready to forgive us when we make a wrong choice, and even better, He is fully able to help us follow Him wholeheartedly so that we can live in the best way possible!

During Bible times, the people in neighboring countries of Israel and Judah worshiped a lot of false gods. But God didn't want His people doing such things! They were supposed to love and worship the one true God. Sadly, God's people were constantly turning away from God and doing things their own way—usually following the ways of people from other countries.

But God still loved the people! He wanted to warn them of the terrible things that such disobedience would lead to. God sent messengers, called prophets, to tell the Israelites to stop doing wrong and to obey Him again.

One of these prophets was a man named Jeremiah. Jeremiah, like other prophets, had been telling the people that doing wrong things would bring BIG trouble. Instead of listening to Jeremiah, the people hurt Jeremiah because they didn't like his message! But that didn't stop Jeremiah!

God told Jeremiah, "Take a scroll. [A scroll was a long sheet with writing on it. It was rolled up from both ends.] Write down My words." Jeremiah obeyed. He sent for his helper Baruch (BEHR-uhk). Jeremiah spoke God's warnings that an army would attack and defeat God's people if they didn't start following God's path. Baruch wrote the warnings on a scroll.

When the scroll was finally finished, Jeremiah told Baruch to take it to the Temple and read it aloud to the people. Baruch went to the Temple and read God's words in a loud, clear voice. This time, some people listened VERY carefully to God's messages.

One person who listened as Baruch read the scroll was an official for the king of Judah. When he heard what Baruch was reading, he was amazed! He went to the royal palace and met with the king's other officials.

"I was just at the Temple and heard Baruch reading the most amazing scroll," he said. "You should hear it yourselves!"

The king's officials agreed. They sent for Baruch to come and read the scroll to them. When they heard God's warning, they asked him, "Why did you write all this? Did the prophet Jeremiah tell you to write these words onto the scroll?"

"Yes, he did," Baruch said. "Jeremiah spoke the words from God and I wrote them down."

The officials were concerned. They knew the king needed to hear God's warning. But they were afraid he might get angry and want to hurt Baruch and Jeremiah! The officials told Baruch, "You and Jeremiah go and hide. Don't let anyone know where you are!"

After Baruch left, the king's officials took the scroll and put it in the office of the king's secretary. Then they went to see the king and reported to him everything that had happened. The king ordered one of his leaders to bring the scroll to him. The leader read God's words to the king. The king did not like what he heard. In fact, he was so angry that he grabbed a KNIFE!

Every time the leader finished reading a part of the scroll, the king took the scroll from his hand. He took his knife and sliced off that part of the scroll

and threw it into the FIRE! The king didn't care AT ALL about what God said! He wanted to forget about it and didn't want anyone else to read God's message! He ordered that Baruch and Jeremiah be arrested, but God kept them safe.

God loved His people. They needed to know that trouble was coming unless they changed! So God told Jeremiah to write out the same warning again. The new scroll was to have all the words that were on the first scroll and more besides. Jeremiah and Baruch followed God's instructions and wrote another scroll. But the king and his people still did not listen. Everyone continued to do what God did NOT want them to do.

Eventually a new king ruled God's people. The new king ALSO wanted to hurt Jeremiah for telling God's message. First, Jeremiah was put in jail. THEN the king's officials had Jeremiah thrown into a hole deep in the ground where rainwater was stored. And all the terrible things that Jeremiah had told the people would happen DID happen, just like God said they would.

Conclusion

Although it was difficult, Jeremiah kept on following God and telling the people God's message. It isn't always easy for us to obey God, either. But just like Jeremiah, we can have courage to obey God and follow His path, even when it is difficult.

New Testament Connection:

In the New Testament, we can read how Jesus obeyed God—even when it meant Jesus would have to die on a cross! In Luke 22:42, Jesus prayed to God, saying, "not my will, but yours be done." Jesus was saying that it was more important to obey God than to do what He might have felt like doing—even when it meant giving up His life.

5 LEAD
Others to God's Promises

Joshua: Spy in a Strange Land

Scripture
Bible Story: Numbers 13—14:9

New Testament Connection: Matthew 28:18-20

Lesson Focus
PreK/Kindergarten: We can have courage because God promises to always be with us.

Elementary: We can have courage to lead others to God's promises.

Bible Memory Verses
PreK/Kindergarten: "Be strong and courageous . . . for the Lord your God will be with you wherever you go." Joshua 1:9

Elementary: "Be strong and courageous. Do not be terrified; do not be discouraged, for the Lord your God will be with you wherever you go." Joshua 1:9

Enrichment Verse: "Always be prepared to give an answer to everyone who asks you to give the reason for the hope that you have." 1 Peter 3:15

The book of Joshua provides a wealth of encouragement and wisdom for the followers of God. Yet this book is not only about following God but also about leading others to Him. As we follow the story of Joshua, we see a man who is determined to trust God's promises and equally determined to lead His people to receive those promises.

Picture this scene: The children of Israel have recently been freed from slavery in Egypt and are on the verge of inheriting the Promised Land. But, because of their fear, the poor Israelites are ready to turn back to the slavery they have just left behind. They cannot invade this land filled with "giants" and take the walled cities. The conquest of the land seems impossible!

Now, Caleb and Joshua had seen the same "giants" and had inspected the same fortifications, yet they insisted that the land could be taken! Because of their courage and trust in God's promises, they were ready to LEAD these people.

God sometimes calls us to lead others in fearful situations, too. When He does, we have the same words that were given to Joshua in answer to his prayer for help in his great undertaking: *Be strong and courageous. Do not be terrified; do not be discouraged, for the Lord your God will be with you wherever you go* (Joshua 1:9). These words are just as true for us!

BIBLE STORY

Many years ago, Moses led the Israelites away from slavery in Egypt. They were walking in the desert on their way to the land that God had promised them. There, they would live in freedom. But the Israelites had been walking for many, many days. Finally, they were camped in the Desert of Paran—the Promised Land was in sight!

God told Moses to choose men to explore the Promised Land. Moses carefully chose 12 men, one from each tribe (group of families), and gave them very clear instructions.

"Go up through the desert," Moses said, "and into the land God has promised to give us. Find out all about the land and the people who live there." The 12 men gathered the things they would need for the trip, said good-bye to their families and friends, and began their exciting mission! They were going to be the first to see the wonderful country God was giving to them!

For more than a month, the people waited for the spies to return. Mothers and children must have wondered when their husbands and fathers would come back. Everyone must have been terribly anxious, wondering about the Promised Land. *Was the land as wonderful as God promised? Would they be able to take over the land?*

The men finally returned 40 days after they had left. Everyone gathered to hear their report and to see the great fruit the spies had found in the land—a bunch of grapes so big it took two men to carry it! The spies said the land was flowing with milk and honey. They said the land was rich and had lots of good food. Excited murmurs ran through the crowd.

"BUT," the spies continued, "the people who live there are fierce and powerful. The cities are huge, with high walls built around them!"

A shiver of fear ran through the crowd. People began to mutter and complain. They got louder and louder, grumbling about the frightening things they'd heard. Finally, a spy named Caleb called out. "SILENCE!" he said. "We should go into the land right now!"

Caleb and his friend Joshua had seen the same fierce people and walled cities. But they remembered God's promises and knew that with God's help, the land was theirs!

But the other spies wailed, "We can't attack those people! They are too strong!" Their fear affected all the Israelites. Soon the people began saying they wished they had died in Egypt or the desert! They moaned they would be better off as slaves in Egypt and that they wanted to go back!

Moses and Aaron fell facedown in front of the people. Joshua and Caleb were so upset that they tore their clothes. They told the people that the land was very good. They told them NOT to be afraid because God was with the Israelites!

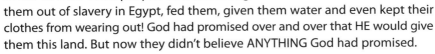

Nobody was convinced. In fact, they wanted to HURT Joshua and Caleb! Moses was heartbroken at the sinful, fearful way the people acted. God had done miracles EVERY DAY for these people. God had brought them out of slavery in Egypt, fed them, given them water and even kept their clothes from wearing out! God had promised over and over that HE would give them this land. But now they didn't believe ANYTHING God had promised.

Moses prayed to God, "Because of Your great love, forgive the sin of these people just as You have pardoned them over and over again since they left Egypt."

God said that He would forgive them! But because the people didn't believe He would do what He promised, the people would have to wait 40 more years. Once the adults who complained had grown old and died, their children would go into the Promised Land.

But what about Joshua and Caleb? God said, "Because Joshua and Caleb have obeyed me without doubting, I will bring them into the new land." And 40 years later, Joshua led the Israelites into the land God had given them.

Conclusion

Joshua and Caleb trusted God and tried to lead others to believe in God's promises, too. When we're at church, it might seem easy to say that we believe in God and His promises. But when friends think we are silly to believe in God or want us to do wrong things, it can be hard to do what God wants. But God will give us courage. And our belief in God can lead others to see that they can believe God and trust in His promises, too.

The Bible is filled with wonderful promises God makes to us. And when we TRUST in God's plans, UNITE with God's people, TRAIN for God's service and FOLLOW in God's path, we can have courage to LEAD others to believe in God's promises, too.

New Testament Connection:

In Matthew 28:18-20, Jesus gives His disciples the Great Commission to tell people all over the world about God's promises. We also read Jesus' promise to always be with the disciples. Jesus will always be with us, too. He will give us the strength and courage we need to lead others to God's wonderful promises.

Age-Level Characteristics

Ages 4 and 5

Physical

Four-year-olds are beginning a period of rapid growth. Coordination catches up in both small and large muscles. They still need a great deal of space and time to explore and enjoy the creative process.

Five-year-olds are learning to tie their own shoes, to cut with scissors successfully and to draw pictures that are recognizable to others. Girls move ahead of boys in development at this age. Coordination has usually become excellent.

Social

Four-year-olds begin to enjoy being with other children in group activities. They want to please adults and usually love their teachers. Provide ways they can sing, pray and talk together.

Five-year-olds enjoy extended periods of cooperative play, usually with one or two others. They enjoy group activities and need to feel that they are seen and heard. Their need for attention may cause them to act in negative ways. Give attention before negative actions occur.

Spiritual

Four-year-olds begin to understand more about Jesus: that He is God's Son, that He lived on Earth to show God's love for us, and that He died but rose again and is still alive. Four-year-olds can also be taught that the Bible tells us ways to obey God and that we can talk to God in prayer.

Five-year-olds are the most likely to respond by talking about the Bible story or Bible verse, and some children will understand that being kind, as Jesus was, is something they can do. Some children, especially those from Christian homes, may be interested in becoming members of God's family. As with all young children, they think literally and concretely and cannot understand abstract ideas like "Jesus in my heart" or "born again."

Emotional and Cognitive

Four-year-olds may often test the limits of acceptable behavior. They begin to ask why and how. Their attention spans are still short, but they can concentrate for longer periods.

Five-year-olds are often able to write their own names, copy words and letters and may even read some words. Five-year-olds can talk accurately about recent events and speak understandably. They love to learn why, still seek adult approval and love to discover for themselves through play and experimentation. Encourage children to think by asking what-could-happen-next and how-could-you-solve-this open-ended questions.

Age-Level Characteristics

Grades 1 and 2

Physical

The term "perpetual motion" may be used to describe children this age. Small-muscle coordination is still developing and improving. Girls are ahead of boys at this stage of development. **Teaching Tip:** Give children opportunities for movement during every class session.

Social

Children are concerned with pleasing their leaders and struggling to be acceptable to the group. Being first and winning are very important. Taking turns is hard, but this skill improves. A child's social process moves gradually from *I* to *you* and *we*. **Teaching Tips:** Provide opportunities for children to take turns. Help each child accept the opinions and wishes of others and consider the welfare of the group.

Spiritual

Children can sense the greatness, wonder and love of God when helped with visual and specific examples. Children can think of Jesus as a friend, but they need specific examples of how Jesus expresses love and care. This understanding leads many children to belief and acceptance of Jesus as personal Savior. Children can comprehend talking to God anywhere, anytime and in their own words; and they need regular opportunities to pray. **Teaching Tip:** The gospel becomes real as children feel love from those who talk about God. Show your faith in a consistent, loving way to model the loving nature of God to children. Look for natural opportunities to talk with children about God's love for them and His desire for them to become members of His family.

Emotional

Children are experiencing new and frequently intense feelings as they grow in independence. There is still a deep need for approval from adults and a growing need for approval by peers. **Teaching Tips:** Seek opportunities to help each child in your group KNOW and FEEL you love him or her. Show genuine interest in each child and his or her activities and accomplishments. Learn children's names and use them frequently in positive ways.

Cognitive

There is an intense eagerness to learn, and children of this age ask lots of questions. They like to repeat stories and activities. The concept of time is limited. Thinking is here and now, rather than past or future. Listening and speaking skills are developing rapidly; girls are ahead of boys. Each child thinks everyone shares his or her view. Children see parts, rather than how the parts make up the whole, and they think very literally. **Teaching Tip:** Talk simply and clearly, avoiding words the child may not understand.

Age-Level Characteristics

Grades 3 and 4

Physical

Children at this level have good large- and small-muscle coordination. The girls are generally ahead of the boys. Children can work diligently for longer periods but can become impatient with delays or their own imperfect abilities. **Teaching Tip:** When playing games that involve taking turns, keep teams small so that kids don't wait long to have a turn.

Social

Children's desire for status within the peer group becomes more intense. Most children remain shy with strangers and exhibit strong preferences for being with a few close friends. Some children still lack essential social skills needed to make and retain friendships. **Teaching Tip:** Look for the child who needs a friend. Move near that child and include him or her in what you are doing.

Spiritual

Children are open to sensing the need for God's continuous help and guidance. They can recognize the need for a personal Savior. Children who indicate an awareness of sin and a concern about accepting Jesus as Savior need careful guidance without pressure. **Teaching Tips:** Give children opportunities to pray. Talk about the forgiving nature of God. Talk personally with a child who shows interest in trusting the Lord Jesus. Use the *God Loves You!* booklet to explain how to become a Christian.

Emotional

This is the age of teasing, nicknames, criticism and increased verbal skills to vent anger. By eight years of age, children have developed a sense of fair play and a value system of right and wrong. At nine years of age, children are searching for identity beyond membership in the family unit. **Teaching Tips:** You have a great opportunity to be a Christian example at a time when children are eagerly searching for models! Encourage children's creativity and boost their self-concept. Let children know by your words and by your actions that "love is spoken here" and that you will not let others hurt them or let them hurt others.

Cognitive

Children are beginning to realize there may be valid opinions besides their own. They are becoming able to evaluate alternatives and are less likely than before to fasten on to one viewpoint as the only one possible. Children are also beginning to think in terms of "the whole." Children think more conceptually and have a high level of creativity. By this stage, however, many children have become self-conscious as their understanding has grown to exceed their abilities in some areas. **Teaching Tips:** Encourage children to use their Bibles by finding and reading portions of Scripture. Help children understand the meaning of the verses they memorize.

Age-Level Characteristics

Grades 5 and 6

Physical
Children have mastered most basic physical skills, are active and curious, and seek a variety of new experiences. Rapid growth can cause some 11-year-olds to tire easily. **Teaching Tip:** Often in coed groups, boys are less aggressive and girls tend to be friendlier. The mixture seems to bring out the best in both genders.

Social
Friendships and activities with their peers flourish. Children draw together and away from adults in the desire for independence. The child wants to be a part of a same-gender group and usually does not want to stand alone in competition. **Teaching Tip:** When you play games that require score keeping, move on to the next round or activity without announcing the score or winner. If the activity is fun and compelling, most kids will never notice the omission.

Spiritual
Children can have deep feelings of love for God, can share the good news of Jesus with a friend and are capable of involvement in outreach and service projects. The child may seek guidance from God to make everyday and long-range decisions. **Teaching Tips:** Provide opportunities for children to make choices and decisions based on Bible concepts. Involve children in work and service projects.

Emotional
Children are usually cooperative, easygoing, content, friendly and agreeable. Be aware that often 11-year-old children are experiencing unsteady emotions and can quickly shift from one mood to another. **Teaching Tips:** Be patient with changes of feelings. Give many opportunities to make choices with only a few necessary limits. Take time to listen as students share their experiences and problems with you.

Cognitive
Children of this age are verbal! Making ethical decisions becomes a challenging task. They are able to express ideas and feelings in a creative way. By 11 years old, children have begun to be able to reason abstractly. They begin to think of themselves as grown up and at the same time question adult concepts. Hero worship is strong. **Teaching Tips:** Include lots of opportunities for talking, questioning and discussing in a safe, accepting environment. Ask children for their ideas of how things could be done better.

Building Relationships in the Classroom

All good VBS teachers conduct classes. They tell the Bible stories, lead activities and keep order. Some teachers, however, change lives. The children in their classes are never the same afterward. What makes these teachers different?

It often boils down to a few basic skills. Teachers who practice these skills find their teaching dramatically changed. Children respond more openly because they sense that the teacher cares.

The skills below can help you effectively communicate Bible truths and enjoy shared experiences with your students. With practice they will become natural and effective ways to build positive relationships with children.

Nonverbal Skills

>> **Expression**—Greet each child warmly, with a big smile—and don't let it be the last smile of the day!

>> **Posture**—Sit at the student's eye level. Join in the lesson activities whenever you can.

>> **Touch**—Touching says, "I like you; you are worthwhile." Look for appropriate ways to build contact with each child through touch.

>> **Gestures**—Nod in response as a child talks with you. Use facial expressions and gestures that indicate interest in what a child is saying.

Verbal Skills

>> **Accepting feelings**—This means listening, sensing the child's emotions and responding with honest empathy, even if you do not agree. Say, "Kelly says she sometimes hits her brother when he takes her toys. Kelly, I know you must feel angry when your brother takes your things." Then discuss the situation by asking, "What is something helpful to do when your brother or sister makes you angry? What advice does today's Bible verse give for a situation like that?"

>> **Accepting ideas**—Accepting children's ideas helps them dare to think out loud, express thoughts and build on their ideas.

>> **Praise and encouragement**—All children need to feel good about themselves and what they do. Look for opportunities to praise children when they have worked hard, completed a task, shared with others, etc.

>> **Open-ended questions**—Questions that require one correct answer can be threatening to children. Open-ended questions ask for opinions, feelings or ideas, not just facts.

>> **Enabling questions (directions)**—Questions that allow children to decide on a course of action will help develop responsibility for their behavior. Instead of saying, "Put the glue on the shelf," ask, "Where does the glue belong?" Such questions build on feelings of success and value.

Guiding Conversation

"Guided conversation" refers to informal discussion that directs the child's thoughts, feelings and words toward the lesson focus. Relating a present experience to what God's Word says can help a child understand Bible truth. Conversation also helps build a good relationship with each child. Children need to feel that you love them and are interested in things that interest them. Express praise and encouragement as you guide the conversation, recognizing each child's honest efforts and abilities.

Here are some ways to effectively guide conversation:

>> Be prepared. Read the information provided in this book for each lesson. Know the Lesson Focus. If you have access to the appropriate age-level *Bible Story Center Guide* or *Teacher's Guide*, review the conversation suggestions. Think of ways you might tailor conversation to meet the needs of the kids in your class. Write down any ideas or questions and keep them with you during the session.

>> Stay with the children as they participate in activities. They need to know that you are ready to listen and talk.

>> Know the characteristics of the children you teach. Be aware of individual differences in maturity. Be sensitive to each child's home situation and plan your conversation to be inclusive of those situations.

>> Recognize and accept the ways that children respond to guided conversation. Some children are quite verbal. Others may respond with nods or other motions. Engage children in a dialogue rather than a monologue. Conversation should stimulate rather than interfere with the child's learning experiences.

>> Spend more time listening than talking. Look directly at the child who is talking. Demonstrate interest in what was said by responding to the specific ideas the child expressed.

The opportunities for guided conversation with children are endless. Prepare thoughtfully and prayerfully before each session. The Holy Spirit will use your words to reveal God's love and truth to your students.

Reinforcing the Bible Memory Verse

Discovering truths from God's Word can be an exciting and rewarding experience for all the children in your class. Some children may memorize easily as they enjoy these activities. Other children may have difficulty recalling all the words but can still clearly understand the meaning of the passage. Be sensitive to the learning level and learning style of each child. Each is an individual and has a different capacity to memorize and recall. Here are some ideas for helping children understand and memorize God's Word:

>> Refer to the Bible memory verse as often as possible. Your natural conversation and discussion during each activity should reinforce the words and meaning of the verse.

>> Ask questions to check a child's understanding of a specific Bible passage: "How would you say this Bible verse in your own words? What are ways this verse can help you at school? In the neighborhood? With your family? What do you think is the most important word in this Bible verse? Why?"

>> Occasionally share situations in which knowing God's Word has helped you. Repeat a specific Bible verse that has special significance for you.

>> Above all, remember that your own attitude toward God's Word and your memorization of Bible verses will have the greatest effect on children as you encourage them to hide God's Word in their hearts (see Psalm 119:11).